CW00469035

The Original Planted-Based Vegan Cookbook #2021

Quick and Healthy Recipes For Everyone incl. 30 Days Vegan Challenge

Anthony Thompson

ISBN- 9798559522005

TABLE OF CONTENTS

What Is A Vegan Diet?

Vegans are those who follow a plant-based diet, which is rich in vegetables, nuts, grains, fruits, and seeds. Being vegan means avoiding meat, fish, dairy, eggs, honey, and all meat-derived products.

However, this doesn't mean that vegans cannot enjoy some delicious food. In fact, there are plenty of plant-based recipes that you can try, and that will show you that it is possible to change your diet without renouncing your favourite food.

Ready for some inspiration? Here you will find all the recipes you need to know to become a professional vegan chef and impress your friends and family.

Is A Vegan Diet Healthy?

Nowadays, vegan and plant-based diets are growing in popularity. Many celebrities and the media have been promoting these alimentary regimens as healthy and environmentally friendly over the past few years, and there is now plenty of delicious food for those who don't want to eat and fish.

However, many people still wonder whether a vegan diet can be really healthy and have benefits for our body and mind. We have investigated this matter and found some interesting answers.

What Are the Benefits of a Vegan Diet?

Research has linked a vegan diet to several health benefits, such as:

- Lower blood pressure and cholesterol, leading to a lower rate of heart diseases. This may be explained by the ingredients used for diet recipes, which are generally low in fat but rich in nutrients and vitamins.
- Lower body mass index (BMI), which is one of the consequences of a fibre-rich diet.
- Reduced risk of developing Type 2 diabetes.
- Reduced overall risk of cancers, as a consequence of a diet rich in legumes and vegetables.

How to Obtain All Your Nutrients from A Vegan Diet?

Many people and doctors are often concerned about the vegan diet, as it may lead to a lack of key nutrients. For example, the majority of food eaten by vegans are naturally low in vitamin B12 and omega 3.

If you want to try the vegan diet, you should focus on always getting all the essential nutrients from all your meals. To avoid any deficiency, you should always try to include the following in your diet:

- **Protein**. As a general rule, you may not suffer from a lack of protein if you don't eat meat, as far as you consume plenty of beans, lentils, and peas.
- **Vitamin B12**. Plants do not naturally supply vitamin B12. For this reason, vegans should take supplements or eat fortified food, such as plant-based kinds of milk, spreads, and breakfast cereals.
- **Vitamin D**. This vitamin is very important for the health of our muscles, bones and teeth. The minimum intake of 10 mcg may be very difficult to achieve through diet alone, so you might consider taking some specific supplements.
- **Calcium**. Usually associated with the consumption of milk-based food, vegans can still obtain calcium by eating tofu, fortified plant-based milk, leafy greens, and nuts.
- **Iron**. This is a common deficiency among vegans, but you can still obtain this nutrient by eating lentils, nuts, beans, chickpeas, seeds and some dried fruits like apricots.
- **Iodine**. Plant foods usually contain low levels of iodine. For this reason, you should use a non-seaweed-based supplement on a daily basis.
- **Omega 3**. Omega 3 fatty acids are essential for our brain and hormonal balance. However, they are mostly found in fish, meaning that vegans should use adequate supplements.

Best Tips to Enjoy Your Vegan Diet

Being vegan doesn't need you only have to eat fruit and vegetables. In fact, you must still follow a balanced diet, and make sure to introduce all the necessary nutrients in your body at every meal. This is one of the reasons why many people struggle when trying to go vegan.

If you have decided to try a completely plant-based diet, here you will find a few tips which will definitely help you eat better.

- Eat a minimum of 5 portions of vegetables and fruit every day. This is an essential rule that everybody should follow, even those who are not vegan.
- To support your daily intake of vitamin B12, eat plenty of plant-based kinds of milk, spreads and yoghurts.
- Always include beans, lentils, peas and other legumes to benefit from their protein contribution.
- Prefer whole grains, such as wholegrain rice, pasta, or wheat.
- Drink plenty of water to keep yourself hydrated.
- Use unsaturated oils for cooking or seasoning your food, since they are rich in omega 3.

Plant-Based Sweet & Salty Ideas for Your Breakfast

Vegan Banana Bread

DIFFICULTY: EASY ¦ CALORIES: 218 ¦ SERVES: 10
CARBS: 33 G ¦ FAT: 8 G ¦ PROTEIN: 3 G

INGREDIENTS

- 100 g (3.5 oz.) brown sugar
- 75 ml (2.6 oz.) sunflower oil
- 225 g (7.9 oz.) plain flour
- 3 large black bananas

- 50 g (1.7 oz.) dried fruit
- 3 tsp cinnamon
- 3 tsp baking powder

PREPARATION

1. Heat oven to 200 C (400 F).

2. Mash the bananas with a fork, then mix them with the oil and the sugar.

3. Add the plain flour, cinnamon, baking powder. Mix well. Add in the dried fruits.

4. Bake for 20 minutes, and allow to cool before slicing and serving.

Vegan Scones

DIFFICULTY: EASY ¦ CALORIES: 346 ¦ SERVES: 6
CARBS: 55 G ¦ FAT: 11 G ¦ PROTEIN: 6 G

INGREDIENTS

- 350 g (12.3 oz.) self-rising flour
- 95 g (3.3 oz.) vegan vegetable spread
- 150 ml (5.3 oz.) soy milk
- 3 tbsp baking powder
- 1 tsp baking powder
- Your choice of jam, to serve

PREPARATION

1. Mix the flour, the sugar and the baking powder in a bowl. Add a pinch of salt.

2. Add the vegetable spread and mix until you get fine breadcrumbs. You can use a food processor to make this step quicker and easier.

3. Gradually, stir in the milk and mix until you get a smooth dough.

4. Roll out the dough on a surface covered with flour. Transfer everything onto a baking tray and store in the fridge for ½ hour.

5. Once ready, cut out the scones with a cutter. Brush each scone with extra milk and put in the freezer for 15 minutes.

6. Bake the scones at 200 C (400 F) for 20 minutes, and serve warm with your choice of jam.

Traditional Vegan Brownies

DIFFICULTY: EASY ¦ CALORIES: 335 ¦ SERVES: 16
CARBS: 31 G ¦ FAT: 12 G ¦ PROTEIN: 3 G

INGREDIENTS

- 250 g (8.8 oz.) plain flour
- 65 g (2.3 oz.) plain cocoa powder
- 350 g (12.3 oz.) demerara sugar
- 250 ml (8.8 oz.) vegetable oil
- 250 ml (8.8 oz.) water
- 1 tsp baking powder
- 1 tsp vanilla extract
- Salt

PREPARATION

1. Preheat oven to 180 C (360 F).

2. Stir together the cocoa powder, sugar, flour, baking powder and salt in a bowl. Pour the vegetable oil, vanilla extract and water, and mix well.

3. Spread the mixture in a baking tin.

4. Bake for ½ hour.

5. Let cool before cutting into squares and serving.

Vegan Almond Pancakes with Blueberry Yogurt

DIFFICULTY: EASY ¦ CALORIES: 224 ¦ SERVES: 6
CARBS: 46 G ¦ FAT: 5 G ¦ PROTEIN: 9 G

INGREDIENTS

- 400 ml (14.1 oz.) unsweetened almond milk
- 300 g (10.6 oz.) self-rising flour
- 250 g (8.8 oz.) blueberries
- 400 g (14.1 oz.) dairy-free yoghurt
- 1 tbsp vanilla extract
- 1 tsp baking powder
- 1 tbsp vegetable oil

PREPARATION

1. Heat the blueberries in a small pan with some water until they burst. Cook until you get a jam-like texture, then transfer to a small bowl.

2. In another bowl, stir the baking powder and the flour. Whisk in a pinch of salt, the almond milk, vanilla and mix until you get a thick batter.

3. Heat some vegetable oil in a frying pan and spoon part of this batter to make your pancakes. Repeat until all your pancakes are cooked.

4. Mix the blueberries jam with the yoghurt and use it to top your pancakes.

Vegan French Toast

DIFFICULTY: EASY ¦ CALORIES: 210 ¦ SERVES: 6
CARBS: 32 G ¦ FAT: 6 G ¦ PROTEIN: 5 G

INGREDIENTS

- 150 g (5.3 oz.) blueberries
- 200 ml (6.8 oz.) oat milk
- 3 tbsp maple syrup
- 2 tsp cinnamon
- 2 tbsp ground almonds
- 2 tbsp gram flour
- 1 tsp vanilla extract
- 1 tbsp golden caster sugar
- 1 tbsp grapeseed oil
- 6 slices white bread
- Icing sugar, to garnish

PREPARATION

1. Heat the blueberries and the maple syrup in a saucepan.

2. In a bowl, whisk the almonds, flour, milk, cinnamon and vanilla.

3. Heat the grapeseed oil in a frying pan. Dip each slice of bread in the milk mixture, then fry until browned and crisp.

4. Serve the French toasts with the blueberries mixtures and a dust of icing sugar.

Vegan Breakfast Muffins

DIFFICULTY: EASY ¦ CALORIES: 224 ¦ SERVES: 12
CARBS: 30 G ¦ FAT: 9 G ¦ PROTEIN: 4 G

INGREDIENTS

- 150 g (5.3 oz.) muesli
- 250 ml (8.8 oz.) sweetened soy or almond milk
- 160 g (5.6 oz.) plain flour
- 1 apple, grated
- 50 g (1.8 oz.) pecans

- 50 g (1.8 oz.) light brown soft sugar
- 1 tsp baking powder
- 2 tbsp grapeseed oil
- 4 tbsp demerara sugar
- 3 tbsp nut butter

PREPARATION

1. Heat the oven to 200 C (400 F).

2. Prepare a muffin tin with cases.

3. In a bowl, mix 2/3 muesli with the flour, baking powder and light brown sugar.

4. In a jug, mix the milk, apple, nut butter, and oil. Combine the two mixtures.

5. Divide the batter between the muffin cases.

6. In another bowl, mix additional nut butter with demerara sugar, remaining muesli, and pecans. Spoon this mixture over your muffins.

7. Bake for ½ hour.

Vegan Omelette

DIFFICULTY: EASY ¦ CALORIES: 310 ¦ SERVES: 4
CARBS: 12 G ¦ FAT: 10 G ¦ PROTEIN: 7 G

INGREDIENTS

- 350 g (12 oz.) tofu
- 2 tbsp yeast
- 2 tbsp unsweetened non-dairy milk
- 2 tbsp cornflour
- 1 pinch turmeric
- 2 tsp tahini
- Oil for frying
- A pinch of salt

PREPARATION

1. Mix the milk, tofu, turmeric, and tahini until smooth. Season with salt.

2. Preheat a medium-size frying pan over medium heat. Grease with oil.

3. Spoon in ¼ of the omelette mixture.

4. Spread it with a spatula. Cook in the frying pan with a lid and cook for about 3 minutes.

5. Repeat with the remaining mixture.

Vegan Breakfast Burrito

DIFFICULTY: MEDIUM ¦ CALORIES: 370 ¦ SERVES: 3
CARBS: 16 G ¦ FAT: 12 G ¦ PROTEIN: 10 G

INGREDIENTS

- 400 g (14 oz.) firm tofu

- 350 g (12 oz.) chopped tomatoes

- 240 g (8.5 oz.) cooked hash browns

- 400 g (14 oz.) black beans

- 10 g (0.35 oz.) freshly chopped coriander

- 1 avocado, sliced

- 1 red onion, diced

- 2 jalapeno chilli peppers, chopped

- 1 tsp + 1 tbsp lemon juice

- 1 ½ tsp onion granules

- ½ tsp ground turmeric

- 1 ½ tsp garlic granules

- 1 ½ tsp ground cumin

- 4 tbsp olive oil

- 1 tsp hot sauce

- Salt and pepper

- Chopped coriander, to serve

PREPARATION

1. Preheat a pan over high heat and grease with 2 tbsp oil.

2. Add in the tofu and season with salt and pepper. Cook for 10 minutes, or until it is browned.

3. Stir in garlic and onion granules, lemon juice, turmeric, and remaining oil. Cook for a few more minutes.

4. Heat some more oil in a saucepan. Cook the jalapenos and onion until softened.

5. Add in the garlic and fry until fragrant. Add cumin and tomatoes, and cook until it all becomes saucy. Season with additional salt, if necessary, and add lemon juice and coriander.

6. Add in the beans and keep cooking and stirring occasionally.

7. When you are ready to serve, place the hash browns into your plate. Follow with a scoop of beans mixture and tofu scramble.

8. Top with avocado slices. Squeeze additional lemon juice and sprinkle some fresh coriander to garnish. Serve with hot sauce, if desired.

Delicious Plant-Based Main Meals

Vegan Burgers

DIFFICULTY: EASY ¦ CALORIES: 190 ¦ SERVES: 4
CARBS: 21 G ¦ FAT: 8 G ¦ PROTEIN: 6 G

INGREDIENTS

- 1 can chickpeas, drained
- 1 shallot, chopped
- 1 celery stick, chopped
- 1 tbsp tomato puree
- 2 tsp garam masala
- 1 tbsp polenta
- 2 tbsp plain flour
- 1 tbsp oil
- Parsley leaves
- Burgers buns
- Lettuce, to serve
- Tomatoes, to serve

PREPARATION

1. Mash 2/3 of the chickpeas with the celery, shallot and parsley until you get a coarse paste.

2. Mash the remaining chickpeas and mix them with garam masala, flour, tomato puree and polenta. Mix the two chickpeas mixtures together and season with salt and pepper.

3. Divide the mixture into four patties and leave them overnight in the fridge.

4. Heat some oil in a frying pan and cook the patties until brown.

5. Place the patties into your burgers buns along with lettuce, tomatoes, and your choice of sauces.

Cauliflower, Squash and Coconut Lentil Curry

DIFFICULTY: EASY ¦ CALORIES: 482 ¦ SERVES: 4
CARBS: 45 G ¦ FAT: 23 G ¦ PROTEIN: 18 G

INGREDIENTS

- 400 ml (14 oz.) coconut milk
- 200 g (6.8 oz.) red lentils
- 1 onion, chopped
- 1 tbsp turmeric
- 1 tbsp garam masala

Roast Cauliflower and Squash Base

- ½ butternut squash, cut into cubes
- 1 cauliflower, split into florets and cut into cubes
- 1 tbsp oil

- 1 tbsp oil
- Fresh coriander, chopped
- Cooked basmati rice, to serve
- Dairy-free coconut yoghurt, to serve

PREPARATION

1. Preheat oven to 180 C (360 F).

2. Toss the cauliflower onto an oven tray along with the squash. Drizzle with olive oil. Roast for ½ hour, or until very tender.

3. Heat more oil in a frying pan to cook the onion, then stir in the spices. After 2 minutes, add in the coconut milk and the lentils. Cover with water and bring to the boil.

4. After 20 minutes, add the roast cauliflower and squash and cook everything together for 10 minutes.

5. Garnish with coriander leaves and serve with basmati rice and coconut yoghurt.

Muffin Tin Chilli Pots

DIFFICULTY: EASY ¦ CALORIES: 625 ¦ SERVES: 2
CARBS: 78 G ¦ FAT: 21 G ¦ PROTEIN: 23 G

INGREDIENTS

- 400 g (14.1 oz.) chopped tomatoes
- 400 g (14.1 oz.) kidney beans
- 230 g (8.1 oz.) green salad
- 4 medium tortilla wraps

PREPARATION

1. Heat oven to 200 C (400 F).

2. Let the tomatoes and beans simmer in a pan for 10-15 minutes.

3. Grease four muffin tins with oil or cooking spray. Lean each tin with a tortilla and then fill with the tomatoes and bean mixture.

4. Bake for 5 minutes.

5. Serve with the green salad.

Sizzled Brussels Sprouts with Pistachios & Pomegranate

DIFFICULTY: EASY ¦ CALORIES: 126 ¦ SERVES: 8
CARBS: 6 G ¦ FAT: 7 G ¦ PROTEIN: 4 G

INGREDIENTS

- 500 g (17.6 oz.) Brussels sprouts, halved
- 100 g (3.4 oz.) pomegranate seeds
- 50 g (1.7 oz.) pistachios, chopped
- 3 tbsp olive oil
- Pomegranate molasses (optional)

PREPARATION

1. Heat the olive oil in a frying pan and cook the sprouts for 15 minutes, or until browned and blistered.

2. Scatter over all the pistachios and keep cooking until toasted.

3. Remove from heat and add the pomegranate seeds.

4. Drizzle with pomegranate molasses (optional) and season with salt before serving.

Baked Cauliflower in Garlic Butter

DIFFICULTY: EASY ¦ CALORIES: 288 ¦ SERVES: 4
CARBS: 7 G ¦ FAT: 26 G ¦ PROTEIN: 4 G

INGREDIENTS

- 4 garlic cloves, grated
- 1 medium cauliflower, leaves discarded
- 125 g (4.4 oz.) softened salted butter
- ½ tsp rosemary, chopped
- ½ tsp thyme, chopped

PREPARATION

1. Heat oven to 180 C (360 F).
2. Mix the butter with thyme, rosemary and grated garlic in a separate bowl.
3. Spread the cauliflower onto a baking tray. Cover with the butter mixture.
4. Roast for 1 ½ hour.

Sweet Potatoes and Cauliflower Lentil Bowl

DIFFICULTY: EASY ¦ CALORIES: 350 ¦ SERVES: 4
CARBS: 41 G ¦ FAT: 11 G ¦ PROTEIN: 15 G

INGREDIENTS

- 200 g (6.8 oz.) lentils
- 1 cauliflower, cut into florets
- 1 large sweet potato, cut into chunks
- ¼ red cabbage
- 2 carrots
- 2 garlic cloves
- 1 tbsp garam masala
- 3 tbsp groundnut oil
- The juice of 1 ½ lime
- 1 tsp Dijon mustard
- 1 small piece of ginger, grated
- Fresh coriander

PREPARATION

1. Heat oven at 200 C (400 F).

2. Spread the sweet potato chunks and cauliflower onto a roasting tray. Cover with the garam masala, ½ of the oil, garlic and your choice of seasoning. Roast for ½ hour.

3. Meanwhile, cook the lentils in a saucepan with abundant water.

4. Remove the garlic from the tray and transfer to a bowl. Add in the ginger, remaining oil, 1/3 of the lime juice, mustard, and a pinch of sugar. Whisk well, then add in the lentils and stir well.

5. Grate the carrots, add the shredded cabbage, and some chopped coriander. Squeeze the remaining lime juice.

Cauliflower, Squash & Orzo Gratin

DIFFICULTY: EASY ¦ CALORIES: 553 ¦ SERVES: 4
CARBS: 39 G ¦ FAT: 31 G ¦ PROTEIN: 25 G

INGREDIENTS

- 300 g (10.6 oz.) orzo
- 75 g (2.6 oz.) grated vegan parmesan
- ½ large butternut squash, cut into cubes
- 1 cauliflower, split into florets and cut into cubes
- 4 tbsp mascarpone
- 2 tbsp panko breadcrumbs
- 2 tbsp flaked almonds
- 1 tbsp olive oil

PREPARATION

1. Heat oven to 180 C (400 F).

2. Spread the cauliflower and squash onto a baking tray and drizzle with oil. Roast for 25 minutes.

3. Cook the orzo by following the pack instructions. Transfer to a pan and mix with 2/3 of the parmesan and the mascarpone.

4. Chop the roasted cauliflower and squash and add the orzo mixture to the baking tray. Sprinkle the breadcrumbs and almonds, then bake everything for 20 minutes.

Spiced Lentil and Butternut Squash Soup

DIFFICULTY: EASY ¦ CALORIES: 167 ¦ SERVES: 6
CARBS: 23 G ¦ FAT: 5 G ¦ PROTEIN: 6 G

INGREDIENTS

- 100 g (3.4 oz.) red lentils
- 1 l (2.2 lbs) vegetable stock
- 1 butternut squash, cut into pieces
- 1 tbsp ras el hanout

- ¼ tsp hot chilli powder
- Dukka, to serve
- Coriander leaves, to serve
- Natural dairy-free yoghurt, to serve

PREPARATION

1. Heat the oil in a casserole dish to fry the onions until caramelised. Add in the garlic, ras el hanout and chilli. Cook for 1 minute, then add the lentils and squash.

2. Pour over all the stock and bring to the boil. Leave to cook for ½ hour, or until the squash is very soft.

3. Use a blender to process the soup until smooth.

4. Garnish with coriander leaves, dukka and yoghurt before serving.

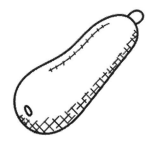

Chilli Tempeh Stir-Fry

DIFFICULTY: EASY ¦ CALORIES: 372 ¦ SERVES: 2
CARBS: 39 G ¦ FAT: 10 G ¦ PROTEIN: 25 G

INGREDIENTS

- 300 g (10.6 oz.) long-stem broccoli
- 150 g (5.3 oz.) tempeh, sliced and cut into cubes
- 2 garlic cloves, sliced
- ½ tbsp gochujang paste
- ½ tbsp toasted sesame oil
- 1 tsp sesame seeds
- 1 small piece of ginger, peeled and grated
- ½ small red chilli, deseeded and chopped
- Steamed brown rice, to serve

PREPARATION

1. Boil the broccoli for 2 minutes.

2. In a frying pan, heat the oil and stir-fry the tempeh for 2 minutes, then set aside. In the same pan, fry the ginger, chilli and garlic, then tip in the broccoli.

3. In a bowl, mix the tempeh with the gochujang and 2 tbsp water. transfer into the frying pan and cook for 2 minutes.

4. Serve with steamed brown rice.

Lentil & Cardamom Soup

DIFFICULTY: EASY ¦ CALORIES: 363 ¦ SERVES: 3
CARBS: 31 G ¦ FAT: 20 G ¦ PROTEIN: 11 G

INGREDIENTS

- 1 large carrot, chopped
- 1 large onion, chopped
- 100 g (3.4 oz.) lentils
- 400 ml (14.1 oz.) coconut milk
- 2 garlic cloves, crushed
- 2 tbsp sunflower oil
- 1 tsp cumin
- Seeds from 10 cardamom pods
- ½ tsp turmeric
- The zest of 1 lemon
- 1 small size ginger, chopped
- 1 tbsp chilli flakes
- Fresh coriander, chopped

PREPARATION

1. Cook the onion, carrot, ginger, garlic and some oil in a saucepan. Stir in the cumin, turmeric and cardamom. Cook until all the spices are aromatic.

2. Stir in the lentils. Pour the coconut milk and some water. bring to the boil and cook for 15 minutes, or until reduced.

3. With a blender, process the soup until you get a smooth texture. Leave some larger vegetable chunks, if you prefer.

4. Season with chilli, salt, chopped herbs and lemon zest.

Lentil Salad with Tahini Dressing

DIFFICULTY: EASY ¦ CALORIES: 460 ¦ SERVES: 4
CARBS: 42 G ¦ FAT: 21 G ¦ PROTEIN: 18 G

INGREDIENTS

- 320 g (11.3 oz.) sweet potatoes, cut into cubes
- 2 large courgettes, cut into chunks
- 2 large carrots, cut into sticks
- 2 medium red onions, sliced
- 2 tbsp cold-pressed rapeseed oil
- 2 tbsp ginger, finely chopped
- 1 garlic clove, grated
- 1 tsp cumin seeds
- 800 g (28.2 oz.) green lentils
- 240 g (8.5 oz.) dairy-free yoghurt
- 2 tbsp pumpkin seeds
- 2 tsp vegetable bouillon powder
- 3 tbsp vegan tahini
- 1 tbsp smoked paprika
- The zest of 1 lemon
- Mint, chopped
- Parsley, chopped

PREPARATION

1. Fry the sweet potatoes in hot oil over medium heat. Add in the courgette, carrot and onion. Season with ginger and cumin. Keep cooking until the veg is tender.

2. Stir in the seeds then, towards the end, add the bouillon powder, lentils, parsley, mint, and lemon zest.

3. In a bowl, mix the yoghurt, garlic and tahini with 1 tbsp of water. Mix this dressing with the lentil salad and top with paprika.

Veggie Protein Chilli

DIFFICULTY: EASY ¦ CALORIES: 658 ¦ SERVES: 2
CARBS: 88 G ¦ FAT: 117 G ¦ PROTEIN: 25 G

INGREDIENTS

- 400 g (14.1 oz.) chopped tomatoes
- 400 g (14.1 oz.) mixed beans
- 1 small sweet potato, cut into chunks
- 1 garlic clove, chopped
- ½ onion, chopped
- ½ red chilli, chopped
- ½ tsp cumin
- 1 tbsp olive oil
- ½ tsp paprika
- ½ tsp cinnamon
- ½ tsp cayenne pepper
- The juice of 1 lime, to serve
- Cauliflower rice, to serve

PREPARATION

1. Heat the olive oil in a frying pan and cook the garlic, onion, and chilli for 2 minutes.

2. Add in all the spices, the sweet potato and season with salt. After a few minutes, stir in the chopped tomatoes and beans. Covers with water and bring to the boil.

3. After 45 minutes, or once the sauce has reduced, the chilli is ready.

4. Season with additional salt and lime juice, and serve with cauliflower rice.

Seitan & Black Bean Stir-Fry

DIFFICULTY: EASY ¦ CALORIES: 326 ¦ SERVES: 4
CARBS: 37 G ¦ FAT: 8 G ¦ PROTEIN: 22 G

INGREDIENTS

Sauce

- 400 g (14.1 oz.) black beans
- 3 garlic cloves
- 75 g (2.6 oz.) dark brown soft sugar
- 1 red chilli, chopped

- 2 tbsp rice vinegar
- 1 tsp Chinese five-spice powder
- 2 tbsp soy sauce
- 1 tbsp vegan peanut butter

Stir-Fry

- 350 g (12.3 oz.) marinated seitan pieces
- 300 g (10.6 oz.) pak choi, chopped
- 1 tbsp cornflour
- 1 red pepper, sliced
- 2 spring onions, sliced
- 3 tbsp vegetable oil
- Cooked noodles or rice, to serve

PREPARATION

1. To make the sauce, blend ½ of the beans with a food processor with all the ingredients and some water. Once you get a smooth texture, transfer to a saucepan and cook for 5 minutes, or until thick.

2. Drain the seitan and absorb any excess water with kitchen paper. Transfer into a bowl and mix with the cornflour.

3. Heat the wok and grease with oil. Cook the seitan. Once ready, set aside.

4. In the same wok, add more oil and stir fry the shallots, peppers, pak choi, the remaining beans and spring onion. Stir in the seitan and the sauce and bring to the boil.

5. Serve with cooked rice or rice noodles.

Vegan Paella

DIFFICULTY: EASY ¦ CALORIES: 497 ¦ SERVES: 4
CARBS: 63 G ¦ FAT: 29 G ¦ PROTEIN: 21 G

INGREDIENTS

- 200 g (7 oz.) white rice
- 500 ml (17.6 oz.) boiling water
- 120 g (4.2 oz.) artichoke hearts, quartered
- 170 g (6 oz.) peas
- 500 ml (17.6 oz.) vegetable stock
- 1 medium tomato, diced
- 1 onion, chopped
- 1 green pepper, sliced
- 1 red pepper, sliced
- 3 cloves garlic, minced
- 1 tbsp olive oil
- 1 tbsp paprika
- 1 tsp ground turmeric

PREPARATION

1. Immerse the rice in boiling water and let stand for 20 minutes, then drain it.

2. Heat some olive oil in a pan over medium heat. Stir in garlic and onion until softened.

3. Add the peppers and the tomato. Cook for a few minutes.

4. Mix the vegetable stock and rice into the pepper mixture and bring to the boil.

5. Add the turmeric and paprika, and season with salt. Let simmer for 20 minutes, or until the rice is tender.

6. Add in the artichoke hearts and the peas and cook for 1 minute.

7. Serve hot.

Harissa Cauliflower Pilaf

DIFFICULTY: MEDIUM ¦ CALORIES: 687 ¦ SERVES: 4
CARBS: 94 G ¦ FAT: 22 G ¦ PROTEIN: 23 G

INGREDIENTS

♦ 300 g (10.6 oz.) basmati rice

♦ 400 g (14.1 oz.) chickpeas

♦ 1 l (2.2 lbs) vegetable stock

♦ 100 g (3.4 oz.) flaked
almonds, toasted

♦ 100 g (3.4 oz.) sultanas

♦ 1 large cauliflower, cut into florets

♦ The juice of 1 lemon

♦ 1 lemon, cut into wedges

♦ 1 red onion, sliced

♦ 1 garlic clove, crushed

♦ 2 tsp sugar

♦ 1 tbsp olive oil

♦ 4 tbsp harissa

♦ 2 bay leaves

♦ A pinch of saffron

♦ 50 g (1.7 oz.) pomegranate
seeds (optional)

♦ Fresh dill, chopped

PREPARATION

1. Toss the rice with the sugar, lemon juice and a pinch of salt. Leave to pickle.

2. Heat oven to 200 C (400 F).

3. In a bowl, mix the garlic, oil, and ½ of the harissa, then add the cauliflower and coat it in the sauce. Spread onto a roasting tin and roast for ½ hour, or until golden and tender.

4. In a pan, mix the bay leaves, saffron, stock, and remaining harissa. Add the roasted cauliflower along with the juice from one of the lemon wedges

5. Transfer the drained rice into the roasting tin and cover with the infused stock. Add the dill, chickpeas, ½ of the almonds, ½ of the cauliflower and the sultanas. Bake until the stock is absorbed.

6. Stir in the remaining cauliflower and scatter the remaining almonds, extra drill, and the pomegranate seeds (optional).

7. Serve with the juice of the remaining lemon wedges.

Spiced Whole Cauliflower Warm Chickpea Salad

DIFFICULTY: MEDIUM ¦ CALORIES: 530 ¦ SERVES: 6
CARBS: 60 G ¦ FAT: 16 G ¦ PROTEIN: 26 G

INGREDIENTS

- 400 g pack (14.1 oz.) chickpeas
- 1 whole cauliflower, stalks trimmed
- 100 g (3.4 oz.) dairy-free yoghurt
- 2 ripe tomatoes, chopped
- 1 small red onion, chopped
- ½ tsp chilli powder

- ½ tsp garam masala
- 5 tbsp coconut cream
- 1 tbsp vegetable oil
- The juice of 1 lemon
- Fresh coriander, chopped

Spiced Marinade

- 140 g (4.9 oz.) dairy-free yoghurt
- 2 tbsp coconut cream
- 2 garlic cloves, crushed
- 1 tbsp ginger, freshly grated
- 2 tbsp coriander stems, chopped
- ½ tsp garam masala
- ½ tsp turmeric

PREPARATION

1. Heat oven to 200 C (400 F).

2. Mix all the marinade ingredients in a bowl and season with salt and pepper.

3. Drizzle a roasting tin with oil.

4. Coat the cauliflower into the marinade, then transfer to the oiled tin. Roast for 30 minutes.

5. Add 100 ml (3.4 oz.) of water and return to oven to cook for a further ½ hour.

6. Meanwhile, mix the spices, onion and chickpeas together. Scatter this mixture over the cauliflower once ready, then roast once again for 20 minutes.

7. In another bowl, make a dressing with coconut cream and yoghurt.

8. Mix the chickpeas with tomatoes, coriander and the lemon juice. Serve with the dressing and some extra olive oil.

Cauliflower Mac & Cheese

DIFFICULTY: MEDIUM ¦ CALORIES: 898 ¦ SERVES: 2
CARBS: 78 G ¦ FAT: 45 G ¦ PROTEIN: 39 G

INGREDIENTS

- 300 g (10.6 oz.) macaroni
- 50 g (1.7 oz.) plain flour
- 50 g (1.7 oz.) dairy-free butter
- 140 g (4.9 oz.) grated vegan cheddar
- 2 tsp mustard powder
- 700 ml (24.7 oz.) soy milk
- 50 (1.7 oz.) macadamia nuts, chopped
- 50 g (1.7 oz.) dairy-free parmesan
- 1 cauliflower, cut into small florets
- Fresh thyme, leaves picked
- 1 tbsp olive oil

PREPARATION

1. Heat oven to 190 C (380 F). spread the cauliflower florets on a baking tray and season with salt, oil, and ½ of the thyme. Roast for 20 minutes, or until browned and softened.

2. Bring a pan of salted water to the boil and cook all the macaroni.

3. In another saucepan, melt the butter and stir in the mustard powder and the flour. Whisk well until you get a smooth sauce. Stir in the cheese and keep whisking.

4. Once the macaroni are ready, mix them with the cauliflower and the sauce. Transfer to the baking tray, top with additional vegan parmesan and the macadamia nuts. Bake for 20 minutes.

Vegan Lasagne

DIFFICULTY: MEDIUM ¦ CALORIES: 530 ¦ SERVES: 6
CARBS: 60 G ¦ FAT: 16 G ¦ PROTEIN: 26 G

INGREDIENTS

- 30 g (1.05 oz.) dried porcini mushrooms
- 900 ml (31.7 oz.) soy milk
- 6 tbsp plain flour
- 1 whole nutmeg
- 4 garlic cloves, sliced
- 2 carrots, chopped
- 1 onion, chopped
- 1 tsp tomato puree
- 2 celery sticks, chopped
- 6 tbsp olive oil
- 250 g (8.8 oz.) dried green lentils
- 250 g (8.8 oz.) chestnut mushrooms, chopped
- 250 g (8.8 oz.) portobello mushrooms, sliced
- 100 ml (3.4 oz.) vegan red wine (optional)
- 1 tsp soy sauce
- 1 tsp Marmite
- 2 sprigs of thyme
- 12 lasagne sheets

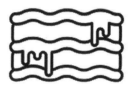

PREPARATION

1. Leave the dried porcini in boiling water for 10 minutes. Once ready, chop the mushrooms and set the stock aside.

2. Heat the olive oil in a saucepan, and cook the onion, celery, and carrot. Season with salt.

3. Add in the thyme and garlic, then the tomato puree. Pour the red wine (if using), and cook until reduced.

4. Stir in the lentils, tomatoes, and mushroom stock. Bring to the boil.

5. In another frying pan, heat more oil and cook all the mushrooms. Fry for a few minutes, then pour the soy sauce. Once everything is ready, transfer into the lentil saucepan.

6. Stir in the Marmite and cook the ragu for 45 minutes. Once ready, remove the thyme sprigs.

7. Heat the oven to 180 C (360 F).

8. In a pan, whisk the flour with hot oil, then gently pour the milk. Cook until you get a thick sauce and season with grated nutmeg.

9. Layer the lasagne sheets on the bottom of a baking tin, then cover with part of your ragu. Keep layering using all your ingredients.

10. Add one final layer of your soya milk sauce and bake the lasagna for 1 hour.

Italian-style Roast Cabbage Wedges with Tomato Lentils

DIFFICULTY: MEDIUM ¦ CALORIES: 610 ¦ SERVES: 6
CARBS: 62 G ¦ FAT: 29 G ¦ PROTEIN: 19 G

INGREDIENTS

- 2 wintergreen cabbages, leaves removed, cut into wedges
- 100 ml (3.4 oz.) extra virgin olive oil
- 4 garlic cloves, crushed

New Potatoes

- 750 g (26.5 oz.) baby new potatoes
- 2 lemons, zested
- 1 tbsp olive oil

Lentils

- 400 g (14.1 oz.) chopped tomatoes
- 250 g (8.8 oz.) red lentils
- 2 celery stalks, chopped
- 2 onions, chopped
- 2 vegetable stock cubes
- 1 tbsp olive oil
- 1 tbsp red wine vinegar
- 3 tbsp sundried tomato puree
- Fresh basil, chopped

Black Olive Pangrattato

- 2 slices stale crusty bread
- 100 g (3.4 oz.) Kalamata olives
- 1 tsp chilli flakes
- 1 garlic clove, crushed
- 2 tbsp olive oil
- 1 lemon, zested

PREPARATION

1. Heat oven at 200 C.

2. Boil some water in a pan and cook the potatoes for 10 minutes.

3. Leave the potatoes to cool. Meanwhile, rub the cabbage wedges with oil and garlic, then spread them out on a baking tray. Roast for 15 minutes.

4. Place the potatoes onto another baking tray and crush them with a wooden spoon or a masher. Drizzle with olive oil and season with the lemon zest. Add to the oven and cook for 45 minutes, together with the cabbage.

5. Meanwhile, fry the onions and celery in olive oil for about 15 minutes. Stir in the tomatoes, lentils, stock cubes, vinegar and tomato puree. Cover with water and bring to the boil. Leave to cook for ½ hour, or until the lentils are soft. Stir in the basil and season with salt and pepper.

6. To make the pangrattato, heat more oil in a frying pan and cook the garlic and chilli for ½ minute, then add in the breadcrumbs. Toast for a few minutes, then add in the olives and lemon zest.

7. Serve the lentils with cabbage wedges and the potatoes, and abundant pangrattato on top. Garnish with basil leaves.

Vegan Ramen

DIFFICULTY: MEDIUM ¦ CALORIES: 556 ¦ SERVES: 2
CARBS: 69 G ¦ FAT: 19 G ¦ PROTEIN: 22 G

INGREDIENTS

- 15 g (0.5 oz.) dried shiitake mushrooms
- 25 g (0.9 oz.) beansprouts
- 200 g (7 oz.) firm tofu, cut into cubes
- 100 g (3.5 oz.) ramen or rice noodles
- 2 spring onions, sliced
- 1 carrot, cut into matchsticks
- 1 head pak choi, quartered
- 1 ½ tbsp white miso paste
- 2 garlic cloves, minced
- 1 l (1.75 pt.) vegan stock
- 1 tbsp white sesame paste, or tahini
- 1 tbsp cornflour
- 1 tbsp sunflower oil
- 2 tbsp soy sauce
- Sesame oil, to serve
- Chopped coriander, to serve

- Sriracha, to serve
- Dried chilli threads, to serve
- 1 piece of ginger

PREPARATION

1. Crush the garlic and put it into a big saucepan along with the white sesame paste, mushrooms, miso, ginger, stock and soy. Bring to simmer and cook until the ginger is soft.

2. Cook the tofu in a frying pan, together with the cornflour.

3. Add in the noodles and cook following pack instructions.

4. Add the whites of the spring onions and the pak choi to the broth. Cook until the vegetables have wilted.

5. Serve the noodle in two bowls, and pour the broth and veg. top with beansprouts, carrot, additional ginger matchsticks, tofu, and the green parts of the spring onions.

6. Season with sesame oil, chopped coriander, dried chilli threads, and sriracha before serving.

Vegan Moussaka

DIFFICULTY: CHALLENGING ¦ CALORIES: 533 ¦ SERVES: 6
CARBS: 60 G ¦ FAT: 19 G ¦ PROTEIN: 19 G

INGREDIENTS

- 30 g (1.05 oz.) dried porcini mushrooms
- 150 ml (5.3 oz.) soy milk
- 6 tbsp plain flour
- 1 ½ tsp dried oregano
- 3 aubergines, sliced lengthways
- 1 kg (2.2 lbs) floury potato, chopped
- 4 garlic cloves, sliced
- 2 carrots, chopped
- 1 onion, chopped
- 1 tsp tomato puree
- 2 celery sticks, chopped
- 6 tbsp olive oil
- 250 g (8.8 oz.) dried green lentils
- 250 g (8.8 oz.) chestnut mushrooms, chopped
- 250 g (8.8 oz.) portobello mushrooms, sliced
- 100 ml (3.4 oz.) vegan red wine (optional)
- 1 tsp soy sauce
- 1 tsp Marmite
- 2 sprigs of thyme

PREPARATION

1. Leave the dried porcini in boiling water. After 10 minutes, slice the mushrooms and set the stock aside.

2. Heat the olive oil in a saucepan to fry the onion, celery and carrot. Cook until softened, then add the thyme and garlic.

3. Pour in the red wine, if using, and the tomato puree. Cook until reduced, then add the lentils, mushroom stock and tomatoes. Bring to a boil.

4. Heat additional oil in a frying pan and cook all the mushrooms until golden. Pour in the Marmite and the soy sauce and transfer into the other frying pan.

5. Cook the ragu for 45 minutes.

6. Heat the oven to 180 C (360 F).

7. Cook the potatoes in boiling water until mashable.

8. Mix olive oil with the oregano and brush this mixture over the aubergine slices. Cook for 2 minutes, or until soft.

9. Mash the potatoes with soy milk.

10. In a lasagne dish, layer the aubergines, the mash, and the ragu. Create different layers with all your ingredients.

11. Bake for 35 minutes.

Vegan Bolognese

DIFFICULTY: CHALLENGING ¦ CALORIES: 599 ¦ SERVES: 3
CARBS: 97 G ¦ FAT: 8 G ¦ PROTEIN: 25 G

INGREDIENTS

- 15 g (0.5 oz.) dried porcini mushrooms
- 270 g (9.5 oz.) spaghetti
- 400 g (14 oz.) whole plum tomatoes
- 125 g (4.5 oz.) dried green lentils
- 125 g (4.5 oz.) portobello mushrooms, sliced
- 125 g (4.5 oz.) chestnut mushrooms, chopped
- ½ tsp Marmite
- ½ tsp soy sauce
- ½ onion, chopped
- 1 celery stick, chopped
- 1 carrot, chopped
- 2 thyme sprigs
- 2 garlic cloves, sliced
- 1 tsp tomato puree
- 1 ½ tbsp olive oil

- 50 ml (1.7 oz.) vegan red wine (optional)
- Fresh basil leaves, to garnish

PREPARATION

1. Immerse the dried porcini in boiling water and leave until hydrated.

2. Heat 1 tbsp oil into a saucepan. Stir in the carrot, onion, and celery. Season with salt and cook for 10 minutes, or until soft.

3. Remove the porcini from water and save the liquid for later. Chop the mushrooms.

4. Add thyme and garlic into your pan. After 1 minute, stir in the tomato puree and the red wine (if using). Cook until reduced.

5. Add the tomatoes, lentils, and pour the mushroom stock.

6. Bring everything to the boil and leave to simmer.

7. Meanwhile, grease a large frying pan with remaining oil. Add in all your mushrooms and fry until they are golden brown.

8. Pour the soy sauce and stir well. Transfer the mixture into the lentil pot.

9. Stir in the Marmite and leave this vegan ragu to simmer for 30 minutes. Add extra water if necessary. Once ready, remove the thyme sprigs.

10. Cook the spaghetti in salted water until al dente. Toss the pasta in the ragu, and use a bit of its cooking water to make the sauce thicker.

11. Top with fresh basil before serving.

Cauliflower Crust Pizza

DIFFICULTY: CHALLENGING ¦ CALORIES: 463 ¦ SERVES: 4
CARBS: 12 G ¦ FAT: 33 G ¦ PROTEIN: 26 G

INGREDIENTS

- 100 g (3.4 oz.) ground almonds
- 1 large cauliflower, stalks trimmed, cut into chunks

- 2 eggs, beaten
- 1 tbsp dried oregano

Topping

- 230 g (8.1 oz.) chopped tomatoes
- 125 g (2.2 oz.) dairy-free mozzarella
- 25 g (0.9 oz.) vegan parmesan
- ½ large aubergine, sliced into long strips
- 1 garlic clove, crushed
- 1 tbsp tomato puree
- 1 small red onion, cut into wedges
- 2 tbsp olive oil
- Fresh basil, leaves picked
- 1 tbsp chilli flakes

PREPARATION

1. Heat the oven to 200 C (400 F).

2. Blitz the cauliflower in the food processor, until you get a rice-like texture. Transfer to a bowl and microwave for 5 minutes, or until softened. Leave to cool, then, using a tea towel, squeeze the excess liquid.

3. in a bowl, mix the cauliflower with the eggs, almonds, oregano and seasoning.

4. Prepare a baking tray and spread the cauliflower mixture over it. Make a thick layer, creating a crust. Bake for 20 minutes or until golden.

5. Meanwhile, brush the aubergines slices with oil and cook for 5 minutes, or until softened. Transfer to another plate and repeat the same process with the onions.

6. To make the tomato sauce, mix the garlic, tomato puree, canned tomatoes and seasoning and process with the blender until smooth. Transfer to a saucepan, bring to a simmer and cook until thick. Stir in ½ of the basil leaves.

7. When the cauliflower base is ready, leave it to cool. Reheat the oven to 240 C (480 F).

8. Spread the tomato sauce over the cauliflower base and drizzle with the vegan parmesan. Garnish with onion, aubergines and mozzarella. Scatter some chilli flakes and cook for 10 minutes.

30 DAYS VEGAN CHALLENGE

DAY 1

Breakfast: Vegan Omelette (See page 20)

Lunch: Jackfruit Bolognese with Vegan Parmesan

DIFFICULTY: MEDIUM ¦ CALORIES: 586 ¦ SERVES: 4
CARBS: 90 G ¦ FAT: 11 G ¦ PROTEIN: 23 G

INGREDIENTS

- 350 g (12.3 oz.) carrots, chopped
- 400 g (14 oz.) jackfruit in water, drained and chopped
- 350 g (12.3 oz.) wholemeal spaghetti
- 4 tsp vegetable bouillon powder

- 100 g (3.5 oz.) red lentils
- 4 garlic cloves, grated
- 4 celery sticks, chopped
- 1 tbsp rapeseed oil
- 3 tbsp tomato puree
- Chopped parsley, to serve

Vegan Parmesan

- 40 g (1.4 oz.) cashews
- 1 tsp garlic granules
- 4 tsp yeast

PREPARATION

1. Heat some oil in a frying pan and cook the celery, carrots and garlic for 10 minutes.

2. To make the vegan parmesan, mix all the ingredients with a food processor. Season with salt, if necessary.

3. Add the jackfruit into the frying pan, along with tomato puree, thyme, and bouillon powder. Cover with water and cook for 25-30 minutes.

4. Meanwhile, cook the spaghetti in boiling salted water until al dente.

5. Serve the pasta with the vegetable mixture, and top with the vegan parmesan.

Dinner: Cauliflower, Squash and Coconut Lentil Curry (See page 25)

DAY 2

Breakfast: Vegan Scones (See page 15)

Lunch: Vegan Bolognese (See page 53)

Dinner: Vegan Ragu

DIFFICULTY: MEDIUM ¦ CALORIES: 268 ¦ SERVES: 6
CARBS: 30 G ¦ FAT: 7 G ¦ PROTEIN: 14 G

INGREDIENTS

- 30 g (1.05 oz.) dried porcini mushrooms
- 100 ml (3.4 oz.) vegan red wine (optional)
- 2 cans plum tomatoes
- 250 g (8.8 oz.) dried green lentils
- 250 g (8.8 oz.) portobello mushrooms sliced
- 250 g (8.8 oz.) chestnut mushrooms, sliced
- 2 celery sticks, chopped
- 2 carrots, chopped
- 1 onion, chopped
- 1 tsp tomato puree

- 3 tbsp olive oil
- 2 thyme sprigs
- 1 tsp Marmite
- 1 tsp soy sauce

PREPARATION

1. Immerse the dried porcini in boiling water.

2. In a large pan, cook the carrot, celery and onion until soft.

3. Chop the porcini and set aside the stock.

4. Add the garlic and thyme in the pan. After a couple of minutes, stir in the tomato puree and the wine (if using). Cook until all the liquid is reduced, then add the mushroom stock and tomatoes. Bring to the boil.

5. In another frying pan, heat some olive oil and cook the mushrooms until golden. Pour in the soy sauce, stir well, then transfer to the lentils pan.

6. Stir in the Marmite and leave to simmer for ½ hour, or until the lentils are ready.

7. Remove the thyme, and season with salt and pepper before serving.

DAY 3

Breakfast: Vegan Breakfast Burrito (See page 21)

Lunch: Vegan Moussaka (See page 51)

Dinner: Vegan Jambalaya

DIFFICULTY: EASY ¦ CALORIES: 547 ¦ SERVES: 2
CARBS: 77 G ¦ FAT: 15 G ¦ PROTEIN: 18 G

INGREDIENTS

- 1 large onion, chopped
- 115 g (4 oz.) brown basmati rice
- 1 yellow pepper, chopped
- 2 tbsp cold-pressed rapeseed oil
- ½ tsp chilli flakes
- 2 tsp smoked paprika
- ½ tsp dried oregano
- 400 g (14.1 oz.) chopped tomatoes
- 400 g (14.1 oz.) butter beans
- 2 garlic cloves, grated
- 2 tsp vegetable bouillon powder
- 1 large handful of parsley, chopped

PREPARATION

1. Heat the olive oil in a frying pan to cook the celery, onion and pepper until softened. Stir in the rice and all the spices. Add the tomatoes and some water, along with the beans, garlic and bouillon. Bring to a simmer and cook for ½ hour.

2. Stir in the parsley and serve hot.

DAY 4

Breakfast: Breakfast Burrito (See page 21)

Lunch: Vegan Burgers (See page 24)

Dinner: Vegan Sausage Rolls

DIFFICULTY: EASY ¦ CALORIES: 326 ¦ SERVES: 10
CARBS: 27 G ¦ FAT: 20 G ¦ PROTEIN: 7 G

INGREDIENTS

- 250 g (8.8 oz.) chestnut mushrooms
- 2 leeks, chopped
- 30 g (1 oz.) chestnuts, chopped
- 70 g (2.5 oz.) white breadcrumbs
- 2 garlic cloves, crushed
- 3 tbsp olive oil
- 1 tbsp brown rice miso
- 1 tbsp sage leaves, chopped
- 1 sheet ready-rolled puff pastry
- 1 tsp plain flour
- 2 tsp Dijon mustard

PREPARATION

1. Process the mushrooms in a blender until they are chopped. Fry the mushrooms in a frying pan, then add in sage, miso, garlic, and mustard.

2. In the same frying pan, cook the leek with additional olive oil.

3. Heat the oven at 200 C (400 F).

4. Mix the leeks with the mushroom mixture and then add the breadcrumbs and the chestnuts. Season with salt and pepper.

5. Mould the mushrooms mixture into a sausage shape and place at the centre of your pastry. Seal along the seam with a fork, and then cut into pieces.

6. Bake for 25-30 minutes.

7. Sprinkle with sesame seeds and serve warm.

DAY 5

Breakfast: Vegan Brownies (See page 16)

Lunch: Vegan Ramen (See page 49)

Dinner: Vegan Shepard's Pie

DIFFICULTY: CHALLENGING ¦ CALORIES: 348 ¦ SERVES: 8
CARBS: 43 G ¦ FAT: 11 G ¦ PROTEIN: 11 G

INGREDIENTS

- 1.2 kg (2.6 lbs) floury potatoes
- 30 g (1 oz.) dried porcini mushrooms
- 50 ml (1.7 oz.) vegetable oil
- 1 can chickpeas
- 300 g (10.6 oz.) frozen spinach
- 300 g (10.6 oz.) frozen peas
- 4 celery sticks, chopped
- 2 large leeks, chopped
- 1 small butternut squash, cut into cubes
- 4 medium carrots, cut into cubes
- 2 onions, chopped
- 3 garlic cloves, crushed
- 2 tsp smoked paprika
- 2 tbsp tomato puree
- 1 vegetable stock cube
- 30 ml (1 oz.) olive oil
- Oregano, chopped
- Sage, chopped
- Thyme, leaves picked
- Parsley, chopped
- Tomato ketchup, to serve

PREPARATION

1. Soak the dried porcini in hot water for 15 minutes. Then drain them but reserve the stock.

2. Place the potatoes in a saucepan, cover with water and bring to a boil. Cook for 40 minutes.

3. Meanwhile, heat the olive oil in a frying pan to cook the onions, mushrooms, carrots, and leeks. Add the stock cube and cook until the vegetables are soft.

4. Add in the paprika, tomato puree, garlic, herbs and squash. After a few minutes, increase the heat and add the celery.

5. Add the chickpeas with their water and the mushroom stock. Keep stirring and tip in the frozen spinach and peas.

6. Peel the potatoes and mash ¼ of them with a fork, then stir into the vegetables. Cut the remaining potatoes into chunks and season with parsley and olive oil.

7. Heat oven at 200 C (400 F).

8. Bake the mushrooms and potatoes filling for 45 minutes

9. Serve with tomato ketchup.

DAY 6

Breakfast: Vegan Almond Pancakes with Blueberry Yogurt (See page 17)

Lunch: Vegan Lasagne (See page 45)

Dinner: Orange and Mint Salad

DIFFICULTY: EASY ¦ CALORIES: 222 ¦ SERVES: 4
CARBS: 54 G ¦ FAT: 1 G ¦ PROTEIN: 4 G

INGREDIENTS

- 4 large oranges, peeled
- 1 tbsp rose syrup
- 1 small bunch mint, chopped
- 12 soft dates, sliced lengthways

PREPARATION

1. Place the oranges in a bowl and add the chopped mint and the dates.

2. Pour the rose syrup and mix well.

3. Serve the salad in a small bowl with additional mint leaves.

Breakfast: Vegan Banana Bread (See page 14)

Lunch: Spinach & Chickpeas Curry

DIFFICULTY: EASY ¦ CALORIES: 203 ¦ SERVES: 4
CARBS: 28 G ¦ FAT: 4 G ¦ PROTEIN: 9 G

INGREDIENTS

- 400 g (14.1 oz.) cherry tomatoes
- 250 g (8.8 oz.) baby leaf spinach
- 400 g (14.1 oz.) chickpeas
- 1 onion, chopped
- 2 tbsp mild curry paste
- Cooked basmati rice, to serve

PREPARATION

1. Heat the curry paste in a frying pan. After a few minutes, add the onion and cook until softened. Stir in the tomatoes and cook until the sauce has reduced.

2. Add the chickpeas and season well. Once ready, tip in the baby leaf spinach and stir well.

3. Season with extra salt and lemon juice, then serve with cooked basmati rice.

Dinner: Vegan Paella (See page 39)

DAY 8

Breakfast: Vegan Omelette (See page 20)

Lunch: Vegan Chilli

DIFFICULTY: EASY ¦ CALORIES: 367 ¦ SERVES: 4
CARBS: 48 G ¦ FAT: 10 G ¦ PROTEIN: 12 G

INGREDIENTS

- 2 sweet potatoes, cut into chunks
- 2 carrots, chopped
- 1 onion, chopped
- 1 red pepper, cut into chunks
- 2 garlic cloves, crushed
- 2 celery sticks, chopped
- 2 tsp ground cumin
- 2 tsp smoked paprika
- 3 tbsp olive oil
- 2 tsp chilli powder
- 1 tbsp tomato puree
- 1 tsp dried oregano
- 1 can chopped tomatoes
- 1 can kidney beans, drained
- 1 can black beans, drained

- Lime wedge, to serve
- Guacamole, to serve
- Cooked rice, to serve

PREPARATION

1. Preheat the oven to 200 C (400 F).

2. Place the sweet potatoes chunks in a roasting tin, and drizzle with oil. Season with ground cumin and smoked paprika. Mix everything, then add additional salt and pepper. Roast for 25 minutes.

3. Meanwhile, grease a frying pan with some oil to cook the carrot, celery and onion until softened. Add extra ground cumin and smoked paprika, then stir in the tomato puree.

4. Add the chopped tomatoes and red pepper, and some water. Bring to a boil and cook for 20 minutes.

5. Add the beans and cook for additional 10 minutes, then add the sweet potatoes.

6. Serve with lime wedges, rice, guacamole and fresh coriander (optional).

Dinner: Italian-style Roast Cabbage Wedges
with Tomato Lentils (See page 47)

DAY 9

Breakfast: Chia and Almond Overnight Oats

DIFFICULTY: EASY ¦ CALORIES: 370 ¦ SERVES: 4
CARBS: 38 G ¦ FAT: 15 G ¦ PROTEIN: 14 G

INGREDIENTS

- 200 g (6.8 oz.) porridge oats
- 600 ml (21 oz.) unsweetened almond milk
- 125 g (4.4 oz.) punnet raspberries
- 2 tsp vanilla extract
- 50 g (1.7 oz.) chia seeds
- 100 g (3.7 oz.) almond yoghurt
- 20 g (0.7 oz.) flaked almonds, toasted
- 250 g (8.8 oz.) punnet blueberries

PREPARATION

1. Mix the oats and seeds in a bowl. Pour the milk and the vanilla extract.
2. Add the raspberries into the mixture and crush them with a fork.
3. Serve the oats mixture into four bowls, and top with yoghurt and additional berries.
4. Cover and let chill overnight.
5. Serve with additional almond milk and flaked almonds.

Lunch: Vegan Moussaka (See page 51)

Dinner: Cauliflower, Squash and Coconut Lentil Curry (See page 25)

DAY 10

Breakfast: Slow Cooker Breakfast Beans

DIFFICULTY: EASY ¦ CALORIES: 149 ¦ SERVES: 4
CARBS: 21 G ¦ FAT: 3 G ¦ PROTEIN: 6 G

INGREDIENTS

- 200 ml (6.8 oz.) passata
- 1 can pinto beans, drained
- 1 onion, sliced
- 1 tbsp white wine vinegar
- 1 tbsp olive oil
- 2 garlic cloves, chopped
- 1 small bunch coriander, chopped

PREPARATION

1. Heat some oil in a frying pan, and fry the onions. Add in the garlic, sugar, and vinegar.

2. Stir in the passata and the beans. Season with salt and pepper.

3. Transfer everything into the slow cooker, and cook on low for 5 hours.

Lunch: Muffin Tin Chilli Pots (See page 27)

Dinner: Lentil & Cardamom Soup (See page 34)

DAY 11

Breakfast: Vegan Breakfast Muffins (See page 19)

Lunch: Cauliflower, Paneer & Pea Curry

DIFFICULTY: EASY ¦ CALORIES: 321 ¦ SERVES: 4
CARBS: 21 G ¦ FAT: 14 G ¦ PROTEIN: 21 G

INGREDIENTS

- 225 g (7.9 oz.) paneer, cut into cubes
- 500 g (1.1 lbs) passata
- 200 g (6.8 oz.) frozen peas
- 2 onions, sliced
- 1 head of cauliflower, broken into florets
- 1 tbsp sunflower oil
- 2 tbsp tikka masala paste
- Fresh coriander, chopped
- Cooked basmati rice or naan bread, to serve
- Your choice of chutney, to serve

PREPARATION

1. Heat some oil in a frying pan and fry the paneer until crisp, then set aside.

2. In the same pan, cook the cauliflower with the onions until softener. Stir in the curry paste and garlic, and cover with the passata and some water. bring to a simmer and cook for 20 minutes.

3. Add the crispy paneer back to the pan, along with the frozen peas. Stir in 2/3 of the coriander.

4. Once ready, serve with the remaining coriander, your choice of chutney, naan bread or basmati rice.

Dinner: Spiced whole cauliflower & warm chickpea salad (See page 42)

DAY 12

Breakfast: Chive Waffles with Maple & Soy Mushrooms

DIFFICULTY: EASY ¦ CALORIES: 227 ¦ SERVES: 6
CARBS: 30 G ¦ FAT: 8 G ¦ PROTEIN: 7 G

INGREDIENTS

- 500 ml (17.6 oz.) soy milk

- 150 g (5.3 oz.) polenta

- 100 g (3.4 oz.) cooked, mashed sweet potatoes

- 130 g (4.6 oz.) plain flour

- 2 tbsp rapeseed oil

- 1 tsp cider vinegar

- 1 tbsp maple syrup

- 1 tbsp baking powder

- 6 large mushrooms, sliced

- 2 tsp light soy sauce

- 1 small bunch chives, snipped

- 1 tbsp olive oil

- Soy yoghurt, to serve

PREPARATION

1. Heat your waffle iron.

2. In a bowl, mix the soy milk with the rapeseed oil, vinegar, and sweet potato mash.

3. In another bowl, mix the flour, polenta, and baking powder. Season with salt. Gently pour the milk mixture and whisk until you get a batter. Add ½ of the chives.

4. Pour part of the batter into the waffle iron and cook for 5 minutes. Repeat until you have all your waffles.

5. Mix the soy sauce with the maple syrup and brush this mixture over the mushrooms. Fry the mushrooms in olive oil until browned.

6. Serve the waffles with mushrooms, soy yoghurt, and top with the remaining chives.

Lunch: Muffin Tin Chilli Pots (See page 27)

Dinner: Lentil salad with tahini dressing (See page 35)

DAY 13

Breakfast: Vegan Scones (See page 15)

Lunch: Spice-Crusted Tofu with Kumquat Radish Salad

DIFFICULTY: EASY ¦ CALORIES: 528 ¦ SERVES: 2
CARBS: 24 G ¦ FAT: 33 G ¦ PROTEIN: 27 G

INGREDIENTS

- 200 g (6.8 oz.) firm tofu
- 100 g (3.4 oz.) sugar snap peas
- 200 g (6.8 oz.) Tenderstem broccoli
- 3 kumquats, sliced
- 4 radishes, sliced
- 2 spring onions, chopped

Dressing

- 2 tbsp Yuzu or lime juice
- 2 tbsp soy sauce
- 1 shallot, diced
- 1 tsp golden caster sugar
- 1 tsp grated ginger

- 1 tbsp Japanese shichimi togarashi spice mix
- 1 tbsp sesame oil
- ½ tbsp cornflour
- 1 tbsp vegetable oil
- 2 tbsp sesame seeds

PREPARATION

1. Slice the tofu and wrap in kitchen paper. Place a frying pan on top of it to squeeze all the juice. Repeat until it is very dry.

2. In a bowl, mix the Japanese spice mix, the sesame seeds and cornflour. Sprinkle this mixture over the tofu.

3. In another bowl, mix all the dressing ingredients.

4. Bring some water to the boil to cook the vegetables.

5. In a frying pan, fry the tofu for 1 minute on each side, until browned.

6. Mix the tofu and the cooked vegetables and drizzle the dressing. Serve with scattered spring onions, radishes, and kumquats.

Dinner: Cauliflower Mac & cheese (See page 44)

Breakfast: Vegan Pumpkin Brownies

DIFFICULTY: EASY ¦ CALORIES: 591 ¦ SERVES: 16
CARBS: 37 G ¦ FAT: 11 G ¦ PROTEIN: 22 G

INGREDIENTS

Pumpkin Swirl

- 180 g (6.3 oz.) pumpkin puree
- 3 tbsp orange juice
- 20 g (0.7) coconut oil
- 1 pinch ground cinnamon
- 1 pinch ground nutmeg

Brownies

- 100 g (3.5 oz.) almond flour
- 3 tbsp flaxseed meal
- 1 tsp baking powder
- 70 g (2.5 oz.) coconut oil
- 70 g (2.5 oz.) caster sugar
- 100 g (3.5 oz.) dark chocolate, melted
- 50 g (1.7 oz.) chopped pecans)
- 3 tbsp orange juice
- 5 tbsp hot water
- 1 tbsp vanilla extract

PREPARATION

1. Preheat oven to 180 C (360 F).

2. Mix all the pumpkin swirl ingredients together in a blender until smooth. Transfer to a bowl and store in the fridge.

3. To make the brownie, start by combining the hot water and the flaxseed meal. Leave to soak for a few minutes.

4. Once ready, mix the flaxseed with coconut oil, almond flour, sugar, vanilla extract and orange juice. Process everything in a blender. Add in the melted chocolate, the baking powder and the chopped pecans. Season with a pinch of salt and pepper.

5. Spread the chocolate mixture in a greased tin. Spread the pumpkin swirl on top of the brownie base.

6. Bake for ½ hour, then cover with kitchen foil and bake for additional 20 minutes.

7. Let cool before slicing and serving.

Lunch: Vegan Bolognese (See page 53)

Dinner: Vegan Lasagne (See page 45)

DAY 15

Breakfast: Breakfast Burrito (See page 21)

Lunch: Vegan Moussaka (See page 51)

Dinner: Cauliflower Soup

DIFFICULTY: EASY ¦ CALORIES: 176 ¦ SERVES: 6
CARBS: 14 G ¦ FAT: 8 G ¦ PROTEIN: 8 G

INGREDIENTS

- 100 ml (3.4 oz.) single cream
- 1 l (2.2 lbs) vegetable stock
- 1 large cauliflower, cut into florets
- 4 thyme sprigs
- 1 celery stick, chopped
- 1 onion, chopped
- 1 garlic clove, crushed
- 1 tbsp ground cumin
- Fresh parsley, chopped
- 2 tbsp olive oil

PREPARATION

1. Heat the oven to 200 C (400 F).

2. Spread the cauliflower florets in a roasting tin and drizzle with olive oil, thyme and cumin. Roast for 15 minutes, then discard the thyme.

3. Heat some oil in a saucepan to fry the onion and celery until softened. Add in the garlic, then 2/3 of the cauliflower. Pour the vegetable stock and bring to a simmer. Cook for 10-15 minutes.

4. Using a blender, process the soup until smooth. Stir in the cream and season with salt.

5. Serve with parsley, the remaining cauliflower and extra olive oil.

DAY 16

Breakfast: Vegan Banana Bread (See page 14)

Lunch: Vegan Ramen (See page 49)

Dinner: Vegan Spaghetti Puttanesca with Red Beans & Spinach

DIFFICULTY: EASY ¦ CALORIES: 400 ¦ SERVES: 2
CARBS: 54 G ¦ FAT: 9 G ¦ PROTEIN: 16 G

INGREDIENTS

- 100 g (3.4 oz.) wholemeal spaghetti
- 200 g (6.8 oz.) cherry tomatoes, halved
- 200 g (6.8 oz.) kidney beans
- 160 g (5.6 oz.) spinach leaves
- 1 red chilli, sliced
- 5 Kalamata olives, halved
- 1 large onion, chopped
- 1 tbsp capers
- 2 garlic cloves, chopped
- 2 tsp cider vinegar
- 1 tbsp rapeseed oil
- 1 tsp smoked paprika
- Fresh parsley, chopped
- Basil leaves

PREPARATION

1. Cook the spaghetti in salted water until al dente.

2. Meanwhile, fry your onion in a frying pan until golden. Stir in the garlic, chilli and cherry tomatoes.

3. After a few minutes, add in the olives, capers, and vinegar. Season with paprika and add a splash of pasta water, along with the beans.

4. Add the spinach and stir well.

5. Serve the pasta with the cream and sprinkle with basil leaves and some chopped parsley.

Day 17

Breakfast: Vegan Omelette (See page 20)

*Lunch: Italian-style Roast Cabbage Wedges
with Tomato Lentils (See page 47)*

Dinner: Mushroom & Chestnut Rotolo

DIFFICULTY: MEDIUM ¦ CALORIES: 416 ¦ SERVES: 4
CARBS: 34 G ¦ FAT: 24 G ¦ PROTEIN: 10 G

INGREDIENTS

- 500 g (1.1 lbs) fresh wild mushrooms, chopped
- 240 g (8.5 oz.) chestnuts
- 30 g (1 oz.) dried mushrooms
- 350 g (12.3 oz.) dried lasagne sheets
- 125 ml (4.4 oz.) vegan white wine
- 3 banana shallots, sliced
- 3 rosemary sprigs
- 3 garlic cloves, crushed
- 4 tbsp panko breadcrumbs
- Fresh sage, leaves picked
- 6 tbsp olive oil
- 2 tbsp soy sauce
- Truffle oil, to serve (optional)

PREPARATION

1. Soak the dried mushrooms in hot water. Once ready, drain the mushrooms and reserve the soaking liquid.

2. Process ¾ of chestnut with some water in a bowl, until you get a creamy texture. Chop the remaining ones.

3. Heat 1/3 of the oil in a frying pan to cook the shallots, chopped chestnuts, rosemary and garlic. After a few minutes, stir in the wild mushrooms, another ½ of oil, and season with salt. Cook until softened. Add in the other mushrooms, along with the soy sauce.

4. In a bowl, whisk the mushrooms soaking liquid, white wine and chestnut cream to make a sauce. Add half of this mixture in this pan and cook until it becomes thick and glossy.

5. Heat oven to 180 C (390 F).

6. Cook the lasagne sheet in boiling water following pack instructions until al dente.

7. Spread a generous spoonful of your sauce on the bottom of 2/3 of each sheet, then roll it up. Cut each lasagne sheet in half and transfer in a serving dish.

8. Pour the remaining salsa over the pasta, then bake for 10/15 minutes.

9. Meanwhile, mix the breadcrumbs with the remaining oil, sage leaves and a pinch of salt. Toss this mixture over your lasagne sheets and then bake for further 10 minutes.

10. Allow to rest and cool for 10 minutes before drizzling with truffle oil (optional) and serving it.

DAY 18

Breakfast: Vegan Brownies (See page 16)

Lunch: Tofu & Asparagus Pad Thai

DIFFICULTY: EASY ¦ CALORIES: 321 ¦ SERVES: 4
CARBS: 53 G ¦ FAT: 8 G ¦ PROTEIN: 12 G

INGREDIENTS

- 200 g (6.8 oz.) flat rice noodles
- 300 g (10.6 oz.) firm tofu, cut into cubes
- 300 g (10.6 oz.) beansprouts
- 6 spring onions, halved and sliced
- 10 asparagus spears, trimmed and sliced
- 3 garlic cloves, chopped
- 2 tbsp sweet chilli sauce
- 2 tbsp vegetable oil
- 1 tbsp tamarind paste
- The juice of 1 lime
- 1 lime cut into wedges
- Coriander leaves, to serve
- Salted peanuts, to serve

PREPARATION

1. Cook the noodles.

2. In a bowl, mix the tamarind, lemon juice and chilli sauce.

3. Heat the oil in a frying pan and fry the tofu for a few minutes, until golden. In the same pan, cook the asparagus until tender.

4. Stir in the beansprouts, garlic and onions. After 2 minutes, add the noodles and the tamarind sauce.

5. Serve with coriander, lime wedges, salted peanuts and extra chilli sauce.

Dinner: Vegan Paella (See page 39)

DAY 19

Breakfast: Vegan Banana Pancakes

DIFFICULTY: EASY ¦ CALORIES: 94 ¦ SERVES: 12
CARBS: 14 G ¦ FAT: 4 G ¦ PROTEIN: 1 G

INGREDIENTS

- 1 large ripe banana
- 120 g (4.2 oz.) self-rising flour
- 150 ml (5.3 oz.) almond milk
- ½ tsp baking powder
- 2 tbsp vegetable oil
- Syrup, to serve
- Fresh fruit, to serve

PREPARATION

1. Mash the banana in a bowl, using a wooden spoon. Stir in the sugar and oil, and add a pinch of salt.

2. Add the baking powder and the flour and mix well.

3. Gradually, whisk in the milk and mix until you get a thick batter.

4. Heat some oil in a frying pan and add 1 spoonful of your batter. Fry each pancake until golden.

5. Serve with your choice of syrup and fresh fruit.

Lunch: Cauliflower, Squash and Coconut Lentil Curry (See page 25)

Dinner: Chilli Tempeh Stir-Fry (See page 33)

Breakfast: Vegan Breakfast Muffins (See page 19)

Lunch: Vegan Fajitas

DIFFICULTY: EASY ¦ CALORIES: 352 ¦ SERVES: 4
CARBS: 44 G ¦ FAT: 12 G ¦ PROTEIN: 1A G

INGREDIENTS

- 1 can black beans, drained
- 2 red pepper, cut into strips
- 1 garlic clove, crushed
- 1 red onion, sliced
- 1 tbsp vegetable oil
- ½ tsp smoked paprika
- ½ tsp chilli powder
- ½ tsp ground cumin
- The juice of 1 lime
- 1 avocado, sliced
- 1 small bunch coriander, chopped
- 4 large tortillas
- Lime wedges, to serve
- Dairy-free yoghurt, to serve

PREPARATION

1. Heal the oil in a large frying pan to fry the onion and peppers until tender. Add in all the spices and the garlic and cook until fragrant. Add ½ the lemon juice, then transfer to a serving dish.

2. In the same pan, heat the beans and season with the remaining lemon juice. Season with salt and pepper and stir until the beans are covered with spices. Add the coriander.

3. War the tortillas and make your wraps with the peppers, avocado slices, and beans. Serve with dairy-free yoghurt, extra coriander, and lime wedges.

Dinner: Vegan Burgers (See page 24)

DAY 21

Breakfast: Mexican Beans & Avocado on Toast

DIFFICULTY: EASY ¦ CALORIES: 368 ¦ SERVES: 4
CARBS: 30 G ¦ FAT: 19 G ¦ PROTEIN: 12 G

INGREDIENTS

- 270 g (9.5 oz.) cherry tomatoes, quartered
- 2 cans black beans, drained
- 2 tsp chipotle paste
- 1 tsp ground cumin
- 4 tbsp olive oil
- 2 garlic cloves, crushed
- 1 red onion, chopped
- The juice of ½ lime
- 1 avocado, sliced
- 1 small bunch coriander, chopped
- 4 slices wholegrain bread

PREPARATION

1. Mix the tomatoes, lime juice and ¼ onion with some oil.

2. Fry the remaining onion in extra oil until softened. Add in the garlic, cumin and chipotle paste. Stir well.

3. Tip in the beans and cover with water. cook well.

4. Stir in the tomato mixtures and season with salt and pepper. Add 2/3 of the coriander.

5. Toast the bread and drizzle with some oil.

6. Top with the beans, avocado sliced, and the tomato mixture. Garnish with the remaining coriander.

Lunch: Seitan & Black Bean Stir-Fry (See page 37)

Dinner: Harissa Cauliflower Pilaf (See page 40)

DAY 22

Breakfast: Vegan Tomato & Mushroom Pancakes

DIFFICULTY: EASY ¦ CALORIES: 609 ¦ SERVES: 2
CARBS: 59 G ¦ FAT: 35 G ¦ PROTEIN: 18 G

INGREDIENTS

- 400 ml (14 oz.) soy milk
- 1 tbsp soy flour
- 140 g (4.9 oz.) white self-rising flour
- 1 tbsp vegetable oil

Topping

- 250 g (8.8 oz.) cherry tomatoes, halved
- 250 g (8.8 oz.) button mushrooms
- 2 tbsp vegetable oil
- 2 tbsp soy cream
- Snipped chives
- 1 large handful pine nuts

PREPARATION

1. Process the flour and soy milk with a blender until you get a smooth batter.

2. Heat the oil in a frying pan. Pour 3 tbsp of your batter and cook for a few minutes. Flip the pancake and keep cooking until golden brown. Repeat for each pancake.

3. To make the topping, heat more oil in a frying pan. Cook the mushrooms and then add the tomatoes. Pour the soy milk and cook until combined. Add the pine nuts.

4. Serve the pancakes with your tomatoes and mushrooms cream. Top with chives.

Lunch: Spiced Lentil and Butternut Squash Soup (See page 32)

Dinner: Veggie Protein Chilli (See page 36)

Breakfast: Cardamom & Peach Quinoa Porridge

DIFFICULTY: EASY ¦ CALORIES: 231 ¦ SERVES: 2
CARBS: 37 G ¦ FAT: 4 G ¦ PROTEIN: 8 G

INGREDIENTS

- 250 ml (8.8 oz.) unsweetened almond milk
- 25 g (0.9 oz.) porridge oats
- 75 g (2.6 oz.) quinoa
- 2 ripe peaches, cut into slices
- 4 cardamom pods
- 1 tsp maple syrup

PREPARATION

1. Mix the cardamom pods, quinoa and oats in a saucepan with some water and 2/3 of the almond milk. Brink to the boil and cook for 15 minutes.

2. Pour the remaining almond milk and cook until you get a creamy texture.

3. Remove the cardamom pods before serving into bowls.

4. Serve with peaches slices and maple syrup.

Lunch: Vegan Moussaka (See page 51)

Dinner: Baked cauliflower in garlic butter (See page 29)

DAY 24

Breakfast: Cocoa & Cherry Oat Bake

DIFFICULTY: EASY ¦ CALORIES: 289 ¦ SERVES: 6
CARBS: 30 G ¦ FAT: 13 G ¦ PROTEIN: 9 G

INGREDIENTS

- 500 ml (17.6 oz.) hazelnut milk
- 200 g (6.8 oz.) porridge oats
- 75 g (2.6 oz.) dried cherries
- 50 (1.7 oz.) blanched hazelnuts
- 3 tbsp cocoa powder
- 1 tbsp chia seeds
- 1 tsp baking powder
- 1 tbsp cocoa nibs
- Fat-free yoghurt, to serve
- 1 tsp vanilla extract
- Sugar-free cherry compote, to serve

PREPARATION

1. Heat the oven to 200 C (400 F).

2. Immerse the cherries in boiling water for 10 minutes.

3. Mix the chia seeds with warm water.

4. Drain the cherries and mix with the soaked chia seeds, along with the remaining ingredients (except the hazelnuts).

5. Transfer into a bowl and add the hazelnuts.

6. Bake for ½ hours and serve hot, with yoghurt and cherry compote.

Lunch: Cauliflower, squash & orzo gratin (See page 31)

Dinner: Vegan Paella (See page 39)

DAY 25

Breakfast: Vegan Scones (See page 15)

Lunch: Spinach, Sweet Potato & Lentil Dhal

DIFFICULTY: EASY ¦ CALORIES: 397 ¦ SERVES: 4
CARBS: 65 G ¦ FAT: 5 G ¦ PROTEIN: 18 G

INGREDIENTS

- 1 red chilli, chopped
- 1 red onion, chopped
- 1 small piece of ginger, chopped
- 1 garlic clove, crushed
- 1 tbsp sesame oil
- 1 ½ tsp ground cumin
- 1 ½ tsp ground turmeric
- 600 ml (21 oz.) vegetable stock
- 250 g (8.8 oz.) red split lentils
- 4 spring onions, sliced
- 2 sweet potatoes, cut into chunks
- 80 g (2.6 oz.) spinach
- Thai basil, to serve

PREPARATION

1. Heat the sesame oil in a large pan and cook the red onion until softened.

2. Add 1 garlic clove, some ginger and 1 red chilli. Cook for 1 minute, then add the turmeric, cumin, and keep cooking.

3. Add the sweet potatoes chunks and stir until they are coated in the spices.

4. Tip in the lentils and cover with the vegetable stock. Bring to the boil and cook for 20 minutes, or until the potatoes are tender.

5. Stir in the spinach, spring onions and the basil leaves, then serve hot.

Dinner: Italian-style Roast Cabbage Wedges
with Tomato Lentils (See page 47)

DAY 26

Breakfast: Breakfast Burrito (See page 21)

Lunch: Vegan Avocado and Chilli Energetic Lunch

DIFFICULTY: EASY ¦ CALORIES: 468 ¦ SERVES: 2
CARBS: 25 G ¦ FAT: 39 G ¦ PROTEIN: 4 G

INGREDIENTS

- 2 large spoonsful of cabbage
- 4 paprika roasties
- 3 tbsp olive oil
- 1 garlic clove, crushed
- The juice of ½ lemon
- 1 avocado, sliced
- 1 tsp cumin seeds
- Chilli flakes, to serve

PREPARATION

1. Mash the paprika roasties with a fork or a wooden spoon. Add the garlic, cumin seeds and cabbage and mix together.

2. With your hands, shape the mixture into two patties.

3. Heat some oil in a frying pan.

4. Fry the two patties for 5 minutes.

5. Top with lemon juice and serve with avocado slices and chilli flakes.

*Dinner: Sizzled Brussels Sprouts with Pistachios
& Pomegranate (See page 28)*

DAY 27

Breakfast: Vegan Banana Bread (See page 14)

Lunch: Vegan Ramen (See page 49)

Dinner: Paprika Roast Potatoes

DIFFICULTY: EASY ¦ CALORIES: 297 ¦ SERVES: 6
CARBS: 36 G ¦ FAT: 15 G ¦ PROTEIN: 4 G

INGREDIENTS

- ◆ 1 ½ kg (3.3 oz.) floury potatoes, cut into quarters
- ◆ 2 tsp smoked paprika
- ◆ 100 ml (3.4 oz.) olive oil

PREPARATION

1. Heat the oven to 200 C (400 F).

2. Cook the potatoes in salted boiling water until tender. Drain them and add the oil and paprika. Season with salt and pepper.

3. Make sure that the potatoes are covered in spices. Then, transfer to a roasting tin and cook for 1 hour, or until crisp.

DAY 28

Breakfast: Vegan Brownies (See page 16)

Lunch: Vegan Bolognese (See page 53)

Dinner: Red Cabbage with Coriander Seed

DIFFICULTY: EASY ¦ CALORIES: 97 ¦ SERVES: 6
CARBS: 14 G ¦ FAT: 2 G ¦ PROTEIN: 2 G

INGREDIENTS

- 2 Granny Smith apples, peeled and chopped
- 50 ml (1.7 oz.) maple syrup
- 75 ml (2.6 oz.) vegan white wine vinegar
- 1 red cabbage, quartered and cored
- 2 bay leaves
- 1 garlic clove, chopped
- 1 onion, sliced
- 1 ½ tbsp coriander seeds
- 1 tbsp olive oil

PREPARATION

1. Heat the olive oil in a saucepan. Add in the onion, cabbage, coriander seeds, garlic and bay leaves. Cook for 15 minutes.

2. Stir in the vinegar, maple syrup and apple. Season with salt.

3. Cook for 1 hour or until the cabbage is tender.

4. Remove the bay leaves before serving.

DAY 29

Breakfast: Vegan Omelette (See page 20)

Lunch: Vegan Lasagne (See page 45)

Dinner: Vegan Katsu Curry

DIFFICULTY: EASY ¦ CALORIES: 1124 ¦ SERVES: 2
CARBS: 129 G ¦ FAT: 48 G ¦ PROTEIN: 37 G

INGREDIENTS

- 200 g (6.8 oz.) cooked basmati rice
- 1 carrot, peeled
- 2 tbsp rapeseed oil

- Mint leaves
- Lime wedges, to serve

Curry Sauce

- 1 onion, chopped
- 1 garlic clove, crushed
- 1 carrot, chopped
- 200 ml (6.8 oz.) coconut milk
- 1 small piece ginger, grated

- 1 tbsp rapeseed oil
- 2 tsp maple syrup
- ¼ tsp ground turmeric
- ½ tsp curry powder

Katsu

- 300 g (10.6 oz.) firm tofu
- 1 tbsp cornflour
- 200 g (6.8 oz.) dried breadcrumbs

PREPARATION

1. To make the curry sauce, cook the carrot and onion in olive oil until they caramelize. Add in the ginger and garlic, then stir in the turmeric and garlic powder. After a few minutes, add the maple syrup, coconut milk and some water. leave to simmer for 20 minutes, or until you get a thick sauce.

2. Slice the tofu in half and then into four triangles. In a bowl, mix the cornflour with water and stir until well combined. In a second bowl, put all the breadcrumbs. Dip each piece of tofu into the flour mixture first, then into the breadcrumbs, until well coated.

3. In a frying pan, cook the tofu for 5 minutes or until golden. Serve the rice with the curry sauce and the tofu. Garnish with carrot ribbons and lime wedges.

Breakfast: Vegan Almond Pancakes with Blueberry Yogurt (See page 17)

Lunch: Vegan Chickpeas Curry Jacket Potatoes

DIFFICULTY: EASY ¦ CALORIES: 276 ¦ SERVES: 4
CARBS: 32 G ¦ FAT: 9 G ¦ PROTEIN: 12 G

INGREDIENTS

- 4 sweet potatoes
- 2 cans chickpeas, drained
- 2 cans chopped tomatoes
- 1 green chilli, chopped
- 1 large onion, diced
- 2 garlic cloves, crushed
- 1 small piece ginger, grated
- 1 tbsp coconut oil
- 1 ½ tsp cumin seeds
- ½ tsp turmeric
- 1 tsp ground coriander
- 1 tsp garam masala
- 2 tbsp tikka masala paste
- Coriander leaves, to serve
- Lemon wedges, to serve

PREPARATION

1. Heat oven to 200 C (400 F). Prick the sweet potatoes with a fork, then roast for 45 minutes, or until very tender.

2. In a saucepan, heat the olive oil. Add the cumin seeds and the onion, and fry until softened.

3. Stir in the green chilli, ginger and garlic. After 2 minutes, add the tikka masala paste and all the other spices. Cook until fragrant and then add the tomatoes. Add the chickpeas and cook for 20 minutes. Season with salt and pepper.

4. Cut the sweet potatoes lengthways and place them on four serving plates. Serve with chickpea curry, coriander leaves and lemon wedges.

Dinner: Vegan Burgers (See page 24)

Printed in Great Britain
by Amazon